GOSPEL POETRY
Book One

Ciaran J. Thompson

GOSPEL POETRY - Book One
© 2016, 2020 by Ciaran J. Thompson

All rights reserved. No portion of this book may be reproduced in any form, except for brief quotations in reviews, without written permission from the writer.

Published through Amazon.

All Bible quotations are taken from the HOLY BIBLE, NEW INTERNATIONAL VERSION® NIV®. Copyright © 1973, 1978, 1984, 2011.

The front cover, with the red poppy is in reference to the 100th anniversary of the 1916 Battle of the Somme. Since that most bloody battle the poppy has become a symbol of death and self-sacrifice, which can represent every soldier who gave their lives for us and for the one person who freely shed His red blood for all mankind.

The lives of well-known British people and events have been celebrated or commemorated in the UK recently and are referred to in this book. The major 2016/17 events include the 400th anniversary of the death of the UK's national poet - William Shakespeare 'the Bard of Avon' (1564 - 1616); the 350th anniversary of the Great Fire of London of 1666 and the death of poet James Shirley (1596-1666); the 90th birthday of Her Majesty Queen Elizabeth II (1926 -) and the 65th anniversary (Sapphire Jubilee) of her ascension to the throne as of 6th February 2017.

Contents

INTRODUCTION	1
Kaleidoscope Calendar	8
The Literary Master	13
An End to Discontent	15
The Great Fire	17
A Great Silence	19
The Servant Queen	20
A Mighty Equalling	23
The Mercantile Locomotive	24
A Letter to Death	28
The Response from Death	29
With Him Face to Face	32
Why Must We Betray?	34
The Golden Lime Tree	39
Now I am Ready for Death	41
COMMENTARIES	43
Appendix 1 - The Bard and the Bible	75
Appendix 2 - The Queen and the King	79
REFERENCES	86
List of famous and influential men and women who died in 2016	90
THE GOSPEL	91

Introduction

Dear reader,

I have put together a series of fourteen poems which attempt to address many ideological, philosophical and spiritual matters. The theme of death is one of the main themes of all fourteen pieces and it has no doubt been on the minds of many people in recent years - more so than usual. We have seen it take many forms - from the endless stream of terrorist bombings, knife attacks, shootings and even beheadings to the many deaths of famous people over the course of 2015 to 2017 as well. Death is not something many people like to talk about. It is sometimes referred to as 'the forbidden subject'.

Many of the disturbing and saddening events of the last year and a half can elicit death's companion - fear. Many people are afraid of what is happening in Britain, Europe and across the world. They fear for their future and for their children's future. One wonders about the economics and politics following a major political divorce, which has cut right across the English Channel and will doubtless affect every British home in the years to come.

We are certainly living through unsettling times with constant threats of terrorism and war on the horizon. I myself have been disturbed by all these things and in addition, have suffered several bereavements in recent times.

I believe that reading has the potential to help and to heal. As screenwriter and playwright William Nicholson once said: "We read to know we are not alone". We fear death when there is a sense of loneliness and poetry is one form of reading that can potentially help to alleviate some of that fear. Many seek solace in the words of a poet. Myself included. My desire is that even through reading this collection of my own poetry many will view death in a new and less fearful manner.

Following an introductory piece, I have anchored my collection here with five historical pieces. When we consider the wise words of the revered dead and look back on events which were marked by many deaths, we can re-evaluate our thoughts on death itself. W.H. Auden once wrote that "Poetry is the clear expression of mixed feelings…A real book is not one that we read, but one that reads us…Now is the age of anxiety." (Burton, 2011).

When we express our feelings through writing (however mixed and muddled up they may be) or read the feelings of others through their writings, we can often experience and receive a clarity needed to aid us in coping with those very fears, which seem to so often enclose around our head, our heart and our lives.

As a committed Christian, I believe in the supremacy of the Bible above all other writings. According to *Guinness World Records* an estimated five billion copies of the Bible have been sold. It is therefore, by far the most printed book of all time and it is full of poetry (*Best-selling book,* 2020). In fact, the largest book of the Bible (by number of chapters) is a collection of 150 poems – the Book of Psalms. You are probably family with the 'Twenty-Third Psalm' often read or sung at funerals.

The Psalms inspired and enriched the writings of so many authors - most notably the Bard himself - William Shakespeare, who we remembered especially in the recent 400th anniversary of his death. My poems have Christian themes running through them - namely the message of the Gospel contained within the pages of the Bible. You may notice allusions to the scriptures as you read through my writings, particularly in the lot of four pieces on life meeting death and in the final four pieces which conclude my thoughts on death.

My solid belief is that Jesus Christ has the ultimate answer for everything - including fear and death. Despite being completely perfect in every way and showing those around Him such love, He suffered the cruellest of deaths on a criminal's cross. Yet, He conquered death itself through His resurrection - all for our sake (1 Corinthians 15; Philippians 2:1-15; Revelation 1:8). This brings grace, hope, light and life to an increasingly dark, confused, turbulent and messed-up world - if we allow it to. How many times do we hear people say now: "the world has gone mad?" How true that phrase is now more than ever.

The message that Jesus commissioned His followers to spread is called 'the Good News' or 'the Gospel' (Matthew 28). People often say, "Do you want to hear the bad news or the good news?" and will declare something they've heard as "a gospel truth". Therefore, I felt I should call this book 'Gospel Poetry'. It is not a phrase many would be familiar with -

including myself. Many have heard of 'gospel music', by the likes of Elvis Presley and Johnny Cash, but not 'gospel poetry'.

Perhaps it will be one day considered a new or at least a revitalised form of poetry. I hope to continue a series of these works for many years to come. Even if you do not like my work, I hope you will appreciate that there is much scope in this mostly unchartered genre.

The Apostle Paul once said:

…I remind you to fan into flame the gift of God, which is in you through the laying on of my hands. For the Spirit God gave us does not make us timid, but gives us power, love and self-discipline. So do not be ashamed of the testimony about our Lord or of me his prisoner. Rather, join with me in suffering for the gospel, by the power of God. He has saved us and called us to a holy life – not because of anything we have done but because of his own purpose and grace. This grace was given us in Christ Jesus before the beginning of time, but it has now been revealed through the appearing of our Saviour, Christ Jesus, who has destroyed death and has brought life and immortality to light through the gospel. And of this gospel I was appointed a herald and an apostle and a teacher.

2 Timothy 1:6-12

A WORLD OF
LIFE AND DEATH

KALEIDOSCOPE CALENDAR

Once in time, there was nothing.
There was no colour, no light, no dark, no life.
Then, a bang! A burst!
And a brilliance unknown.

Everything exploding. Everything expanding.
The Painter's brush strokes
being fired hard onto a clear canvas.
Splashing streams of elements
on a billion different paths.

Light and mass. Energy and gas.
Swirling and swivelling. Stars spun into place.
Now filling with colours and now filling up space.

Contrasts and hues of all fiery restlessness:
Show a turbulent tinged world below.
How a molten disk becomes a marble!

An aggregate of atoms,
a chain of living beings appear.
All growing and developing here.
All created for a purpose and crafted into being,
and "each after their own kind" -
they show their true colours.

Then Man, once pure and charged with care
of all that came to life before,
soon chose a path which led to war.
Thorns and thistles, struggle and strain
in man and all that lives below.

Blue skies and butterflies,
a host of golden daffodils:
Aside from the artist and the writer,
Of the beauty of colours do people *now* really care?

For every raised up fighting tribe
and every ancient power:
Emblazons on their foreheads, their chests,
their flags, their walls -
the cultural stripes of their own cast.

Rising empires nail their colonial colours
to their masts.
Royal blue regalia decorate their warships.
Scarlet flags caught high on an ocean breeze.

Faith, hope and hatred from all factions.
Sacred temples of pure white stone
now in arrays of tumult.
Lands once free now washed crimson
with the blood of saints.

All people battle for dominion
over one pixel of this planet.
Red armies and white cliffs of Dover,
Emerald isles and orange orders.

"Vote for us! We are the illuminated ones!"
"Vote for the green party"…
"No, no true blue is best!"
A coalition of colours
could never bring them freedom.

From Dark Age warlords to enlightened thinkers:
There have been tinctures of truth
amongst the dyes of deception.
So what is the answer to all this colour coding?

A Rainbow?

Rainbow nation? Rainbow flag?
Rainbow in the sky?
All mean freedom for those involved,
freedom from mistreatment,
and watery destruction. Rainbow virility.

We're lost in a reverie of rainbows.
Held captive in prisms of light.
So, which colourway do we follow
in this twisting kaleidoscope?

The rainbow which defines us all...
The Golden Rule of love and hope.

*THOSE WHOSE LIFE
AND DEATH WE REMEMBER*

THE LITERARY MASTER

William Shakespeare, who's legacy continues 400 years on.

We read that "All the world's a stage,"
so Avon's Bard of words did say.
We have our exit and entrance days;
we are mere actors in lifelong plays.

So Avon's Bard of words did say
we learn our lines for all our scenes,
we are mere actors in lifelong plays,
but we don't know "what we may be"?

We learn our lines for all our scenes
and read our scripts for each new day.
We do not know "what we may be,"
so we strut and fret our hour on stage.

We read our scripts for each new day,
but do not read the final word.
We strut and fret our hour on stage,
until at last we are not heard.

We do not read the final word
directing us through exit doors,
until at last we are not heard,
once we have made our curtain call.

Directing us through exit doors,
we're unprepared - not undeterred.
Once we have made our curtain call,
stage lights do dim in shady murk.

We're unprepared - not undeterred
to rid these props that keep us hostage.
Before lights do dim in shady murk
let's tear this set and shake this stage.

Let's rid these props that keep us hostage;
tear up the script and stop this play;
tear down this set and shake this stage;
or else for us - this world's a cage.

AN END TO DISCONTENT

When I am laid, am laid in earth, may my wrongs create, no trouble,
no trouble in, in thy breast. Remember me, remember me,
but ah forget my fate...

(Henry Purcell, 'Dido's Lament')

Restoring Richard

Abandoned, crushed,
struck down on Ambion Hill,
I am maligned and misunderstood.
I am your King.

Thrown under soil, more soil, mud,
homes, hardened clay,
people walking on my grave.
I saw it all.

My royal crest reaches out from the grave,
yet it is shattered,
shattered in the minds of men.
They do not think.

I am misshapen, in writhed form...then,
strange mechanical things
move to and fro above.
Five hundred years.

Now, I feel bodies moving closer
and closer still,
wanting to find me and lift me up.
Hands in my grave.

A wicked man of many sorrows
and much peril in life,
and in death, until now.
Now they can see.

All of England do honour me
with my Kingly burial,
and I am lowered, lowered in restful ease.
I am laid in Earth.

THE GREAT FIRE

"...In this calamitous condition I returned with a sad heart to my house, blessing and adoring the distinguishing mercy of God to me and mine, who in the midst of all this ruin was like Lot, in my little Zoar, safe and sound..."

(An extract from Sir Samuel Pepys' 5th September 1666 entry about the Great Fire of London, from one of the world's most celebrated diaries)

Before them - the fire devours,
behind them - a timber wood waste.
Oh the horror which flames empower;
rich and poor, together make haste.

Behind them - a timber wood waste;
it nurtured this malicious flame.
Rich and poor, together make haste,
to London all - this fire came.

It nurtured this malicious flame,
from bakery to church steeple.
To London all - this fire came.
Now I leave with pitied people.

From bakery to church steeple:
so these foul flames of Hell travel.
Now I leave with pitied people,
under smoked skies of black gravel.

So these foul flames of Hell travel,
not the fine flames of wonted fire.
Under smoked skies of black gravel,
the city burns in Satan's pyre.

Not the fine flames of wonted fire,
saw Parliament fall to pieces.
The city burns in Satan's pyre.
London's beauty - it decreases.

Saw Parliament fall to pieces,
all is ruined from river's gaze.
London's beauty - it decreases.
Poor souls burning in the blaze.

All is ruined from river's gaze.
Oh the horror which flames empower;
poor souls burning in the blaze;
before them - the fire devours.

A GREAT SILENCE

For those who fought over 100 years ago in the bloodiest battle in history - the 1916 Battle of the Somme

A great silence spoke *before dawn*,
of taunting terror in everyman
as our spears and guns were drawn.

Nervous whispers to each one warns.
Trench ladders clenched with one hand:
a great silence spoke *at the dawn*.

Then rising up and blazing forth:
colossal flames upon the land,
as our spears and guns were drawn.

The first to fight were doomed to fall.
My voiceless friends strewn 'cross the span.
A great silence spoke *after dawn*.

Then, the roll of gunfire's call
thundered much more than I could stand.
My spear and gun withdrawn.

I look down from rest upon that war,
once fought on lands where poppies now adorn.
They silent' speak of blood *each dawn*,
where knives and guns were all once drawn.

THE SERVANT QUEEN

"I declare before you all that my whole life whether it be long or short shall be devoted to your service."

(HM Queen Elizabeth II, 21st April 1947)

A poetic commentary of the Royal State Funeral in the Future.

From birth she was enrobed in royalty,
From youth she was cloaked in loyalty.
Suddenly crowned, amidst the emotion
of losing one's father to royal devotion.
What a fine glory of waving so gallantly,
regaling the world from her high balcony.
Royal tours refined to such perfection,
bestowed on her with much affection.
Through the years of pomp and pageantry
there were forays of untimely tragedy.

But none so great as this observation:
as now we stand - as one silent nation.
Her cortège glides before our gallantry,
as a symbol of her royal majesty.
She was our longest serving Monarch,
So that is why I share this sonnet.

WHEN LIFE
MEETS DEATH

A MIGHTY EQUALLING

From countrymen to courtly Kings,
from ploughboys to the ampled Prince:
death befalls us all - a mighty equalling.

Of death's success there is no arguing,
yet life beyond life's death does not all convince:
from countrymen to courtly Kings.

An image of life and death does sing
in clear blank blues of sky's expanse,
of death befalling a mighty equalling.

Life's sky clutters with cloudy things:
blowing in many needless plans,
from countrymen to courtly Kings.

From sunrise horizons to life's ending
the overclouding sky does burst.
Death befalls us all a mighty equalling.

We splash to ground clinging life's things.
from countrymen to courtly Kings.
Yet with nothing we came,
with nothing we leave.
For death befalls us *all* a mighty equalling.

THE MERCANTILE LOCOMOTIVE

Chuntering, chucking, chattering, chancing,
on the train goes through the snow,
shifting, shaking, sifting, forsaking,
nothing can make it slow.

Cutting through the countryside,
it tears the tear-stained tapestry around,
and at the breaking of the morn,
its long, dark shadow surrounds.

This locomotive - spinning its grinding wheels;
gnashing away - every moment it steals.
Its smoke billows out, up and above,
and sends to its death - a tiny dove.

The men it carries towards an unreachable place
are seldom satisfied.
They are cold, austere - blackened by *their* world
nothing can fully gratify.

They move but a little -
engrossed in their selfish cause,
"in this winter of discontent"
and cold war with the poor.

Heads down in sharp grey suits, briefcases,
newspapers - seated statuesque,
not one eye veers from business -
bar one are all grotesque.

They do not heed the warning
that their bloated world of dough,
will come crashing down in an instant -
in a pile of fallen snow.

For who could forsake the knowledge
that lying snow on the floor
will not ever easily thaw -
it is always waiting there for more…

Outside the windows of the train
can be seen the people from *the real world*:
the shaken, darkened faces of men -
wielding, welding, winding and melding.

The burdened-heavy mothers -
with their children clinging upon their backs,
pulling, pushing, planting and plucking,
in their torn, muddied clothes.

They are like blurred moving figures;
pencil-drawings of a weird cartoon nightmare,
unlike the passengers warm on the train,
they *know* the cold in those fields of snow.

Something occurs that has not done so for an age
the train begins to slow...
and the men on board begin to shift edgily
how will they cope?

Snow drifts all around pile high
upon the train's brow,
snuffing out the smoke
and breaking the flow.

The train grinds to a halt -
in a snow drift that covers its top.
The poor outside with external jeers -
the men inside with internal fears.

The raspy voices of all the poor
are now heard as the train stands still:
"You are shameless!...Painless!...Faceless!
We are will-less!...Helpless!...Penniless!

They rattle the train as the men inside
don't know what to do,
'til one man steps forth off the carriage door
saying: *"I will help you".*

He clears the snow with a shovel and sword -
and in the ground a line He has drawn:
"Come on board you weak and poor -
come in peace, there is room for all."

On the train stood stern
the business men of old:
*"We will not have them with us
at the front of the fold!"*

The man: *"I will bring them to the rear
and stay with them all"*
The train moves on,
though a danger would soon befall.

The growing lights and closing horn
of another train on the same track
came crashing head on!
Those saved were found only at the back…

A LETTER TO DEATH

from one bereaved

With every willing heart founded here,
I fight the fear of you - the strike of you.
Whilst fear gives life to you and you to fear,
I'll not subside in desire to be loosed.
I feel the grief of you - this sorrowful place,
as your pointed finger presses plenty.
Your breath, your feel, your veiled face
for no one to see, is well known *to me*.

So on that day when I cease to draw breath,
I will not be overcome by you. For the way
I have faced life is how I have faced death,
with an assured hope of life beyond the grave.
Like fear, your friend and ally, you will soon
fade to nothing - *your* death, your similitude.

THE RESPONSE FROM DEATH

to the bereaved one

When my friend girds you up, you are frightened?
You are frightened, but can be thrilled,
yet you see me as a trap, a trap that is tightened?

When you picture me, I've been a sprite-and
a scything sprite of the unfulfilled,
when my friend girds you up, you are frightened?

But I've been written as an angel, an angel entitled,
I am entitled to possess the killed,
yet you see me as a trap, a trap that is tightened.

Why do you fear me, like a strike of lightning
as the room of your heart is filled?
When my friend girds you up, you are frightened?

I am the paved-out way to the gliding horizons,
so let your tortured mind be stilled;
and don't see me as a trap, a trap that is tightened.

If you still want to escape my graven plight-then
look for a way for me to be killed.
But what I fear is that you'll always be frightened,
and will still see me as a trap, a trap that is tightened.

THE POWER OF LIFE OVER DEATH

WITH HIM FACE TO FACE

I lie here disheartened, disjointed, dismayed.
Yet - I don't sense it. I don't feel afraid.
Bereft of any feeling, I rest - numb to the pain,
until the middle of night, when it awakens me, once again.

A demonic wound has punctured my soul.
In sharpened terror - I lie drowning in dark cold.
It is like the depths of winter's dire,
after the warmth and joy of festival's fire.

I am tugged, torn with every windswept wave
of merciless rain - I curl inside this womb - this cave.
No solace I find - other than a memory,
before the pain, in mother and family.

He was taken from us, yes, taken - why was he taken?
Rivers of blood - I see. Oh, why were you forsaken?
His body lying there. His face appears - I hide.
Oh the pure horror of blood pouring from his side.

Staring down at me, in my mind's eye.
I fail to see why he was allowed to die?
I am sorry, brother - so sorry indeed.
I couldn't help you in your time of need.

But then, out of the mist of grief's piercing clasp
I feel a touch of spring, and then my face unmasked.
Somehow my brother's spirit in me raises me high.
He says "all is well with me, come and see blue sky".

I don't have to grieve my brother anymore,
for He gave His life for all in peace and war.
And now I move out of this bed of pain,
I tear back the curtains to see new life again.

And I have joy! Unspeakable joy!
The veil of my unworthiness lifted and destroyed.
I desire to thank the One who did all this for me.
Or was it Him all along? "For I was blind, but now I see."

WHY MUST WE BETRAY?

Why must we betray?
Why must we kill?
Why must we avenge ourselves?
Is it just for the thrill?

Is it to settle a deal?
Or to get our own back?
What good will it do?
Why can't we just take the flack?

The acquisition of memories
and the pain of the past
both conspire together
so healing fails fast.

The need for possessions:
a car, a house, a neckless.
Fiction becomes reality:
"Mine, my own, my precious."

No room for forgiveness.
No room for love.
Where is the mercy and the grace,
the olive branch and the dove?

Of the wonder of man;
he has doubtless might
to conquer the universe;
his achievements take flight.

Yet there is one thing
he cannot be victor over:
his need for retribution.
Of that he does suffer.

It reties the umbilical cord
around his neck.
It turns him back to a helpless babe
screaming for his own sake.

For many a long battle
and many a human death
have been ordained by the words
of a betrayer's breath.

With blazing torches,
they took their chances
to arrest 'the One'
in the garden of olive branches.

"The one whom I kiss,
is 'the One' they all hallow."
He betrayed his master
and died ashamed - in shadow.

Then came the man
"highly skilled in matters of war"
to commit an act of treason
of the highest order.

Not with thirty pieces of silver,
but with gunpowder and guile.
Yet was tortured by those
he thought so evil and vile.

"And then Mein Kampf,
my struggle, my war
to rid the world
of this low enemy I do abhor!"

"For one thousand years
we will reign in this world!"
Yet he and his wicked army
were brought to no worth.

"Revenge is sweet"
No! It is a poisoned chalice.
So what is the answer
for the cold and the callous?

A single rose and an olive branch
for: every enemy's sins,
from: every human being.
For true beauty is found within.

Yes, it is to be found
even in the most wretched of men.
Yet, we so rarely love
or seek peace with any of them.

We need an example,
to teach us how to love
and leave us with His peace.
He will come as a dove.

Some do say "Why can't the good Lord
rid this world of evil men,
so those of us who are good
can live in peace again?"

But everyone has sinned
and fallen short of God's good ways.
We *all* need His forgiveness
for each of our days.

Our history has shown us
we cannot save ourselves.
We need someone to come,
to save us from our Hell.

Indeed, the good Lord
so loved our race,
that He sent His Son
to die in our place.

That's how much God so loved you.
He took on board your guilt.
In His death and His life,
our hope is surely built.

Our hope for a new Earth,
with no sting of death,
no stab of betrayal,
He destroys with His breath.

Repent of your sins
and love your enemies.
Receive His Peaceful Spirit
and you'll live eternally.

THE GOLDEN LIME TREE

As *I* stepped out, the golden lime tree caught my eye.
It is not the closest tree to me, nor is it the greatest,
but somehow it draws my gaze as soon as I step out.

The rest of the autumn day
appeared laid out before me as a red rug,
as though it was done that way just for me.
I know it was not as it is there for me and for you.

As *we* step out and capture the essence of this autumn in
its late October prime,
it is unavoidably clear
that it is a time of flux and fluctuation.
But that is its strength. That is its wonder.

It is in the never ceasing winds
which blow through the trees
and in the feeling of it
on our brows, hands and cheeks.
It is a gentle gust, yet a blustery breeze.

As *anyone* who steps out in the golden years of life
will know *and* understand - autumn's strength is in
its constant moving, its shifting and its driving.
That is how it prepares for the release of winter.

The wind sweeps more leaves away
from the tree day by day.
But it keeps on moving. The tree allows it to.
It prepares itself for death - which is golden.
For death is only a means to a new life...

...

And so the golden life tree of life waits dead -
quietly in the grave of winter.
Still and steady, bare and bony.
It waits for the oncoming of spring,
when it's roots will be crowned with golden daffodils.

And after it has come upon that reach,
it buds joyfully on its many branches.
Summer comes with a
blaze of heightened sunshine,
lighting up its bows in pure golden light.

The tree freely stretches out -
grasping the fullness of life;
never again to face death,
even for just a season,
as death for this righteous tree
is swallowed up in the light of victory.

NOW I AM READY FOR DEATH

If I were never to see another sunrise
breaking out upon a wide and open ocean,
or if I were never destined to gaze once more
upon a star embraced night laid on a stone wall,
I know that in my heart I would count myself blessed,
For I have now learnt to trust the Companion
who teaches me to cherish every moment
and to delight in the wonder and the splendour
of each new day as though it were my very last.

I am now surely ready for life's great adventure:
the crossing into that undiscovered country.
For I will now never look upon death with fear,
but with the rekindling of hope for this new way;
this everlasting truth - that death gives birth to life.

…

LIFE ETERNAL.

Commentaries

Kaleidoscope Calendar

Here, we begin with a free-flowing, non-conforming poem, which tries to convey a general 'big picture' of life on Earth - its peoples and its problems - using colours (which are universally understood) to enhance the message to the reader. I tried to use a fair amount of enjambment to portray the ongoing story of the planet. It is meant to be a vivid, polemical poem which addresses some spiritual, ideological and philosophical questions, whilst still employing a healthy range of concrete images with which to anchor thoughts in the reader's imagination.

The line "each after their own kind" is taken from Genesis 1:24 and falls before the stanza which explains the partial loss of our connection to the world and to God - the fall of man. This even caused by Adam and Eve corrupted all mankind and nature along with it, according to the scriptures (Gen. 3, Rom. 5-6, 8). However, God promised to one day restore all creation back to a perfect, peaceful state. He will also punish those who destroy the earth and save those who faithfully loved Him and followed His ways (Isa. 11; 66, Rev. 11:18; chs. 21-22).

"A host, of golden daffodils" is an obvious reference to Wordsworth's infamous words. Its approach might also remind one of Tennyson's extremely long poem (or set of poems as some regard it) 'In Memoriam A.H.H', which has over 700 stanzas. Here are just four of them:

Strong Son of God, immortal Love,
Whom we, that have not seen thy face,
By faith, and faith alone, embrace,
Believing where we cannot prove;

Thine are these orbs of light and shade;
Thou madest Life in man and brute;
Thou madest Death; and lo, thy foot
Is on the skull which thou hast made.

...

Who trusted God was love indeed
And love Creation's final law—
Tho' Nature, red in tooth and claw
With ravine, shriek'd against his creed—

Who loved, who suffer'd countless ills,
Who battled for the True, the Just,
Be blown about the desert dust,
Or seal'd within the iron hills?

I was also somewhat influenced by scientist Carl Sagan's (1934-1996) words describing the 'Pale Blue Dot' photograph taken in 1990 from the Voyager 1 spacecraft. The photograph was of Earth, taken from 6 billion kilometres away, causing our planet to be smaller than one pixel. During a public lecture at Cornell University in 1994, Sagan spoke on how the photo affected his thinking of man, the world and our place in the Universe. He shared that it is on that "point of pale blue light" in the immense vastness of space that every man, woman and child has ever lived; "every saint and sinner"; every religious and political power has ever existed and has tried to "become the momentary masters of a fraction of a dot". He also emphasised, "how eager [people] are to kill one another, how fervent their hatreds".

He continues: "Our posturing's, our imagined self-importance, the delusion that we have some privileged position in the Universe, are challenged by this point of pale light. Our planet is a lonely speck in the great enveloping cosmic dark. In our obscurity, in all this vastness, there is no hint that help will come from elsewhere to save us from ourselves." (Sagan, 1994). I agree with virtually everything in his whole speech apart from that final quoted sentence. Why? Because the Creator of our world saw how destructive we had become and decided to enact His plan of salvation long spoken about throughout the scriptures:

> "For God so loved [that pale blue dot] that he gave his one and only Son, that whoever believes in him shall not perish but have eternal life. For God did not send his Son into the world to condemn the world, but to save the world through him. Whoever believes in him is not condemned, but whoever does not believe stands condemned already because they have not believed in the name of God's one and only Son. This is the verdict: light has come into the world, but people loved darkness instead of light because their

deeds were evil. Everyone who does evil hates the light, and will not come into the light for fear that their deeds will be exposed. But whoever lives by the truth comes into the light, so that it may be seen plainly that what they have done has been done in the sight of God."

John 3:16-21
(Words in square brackets replaced 'the world'.
See also: Genesis 3:15, Isaiah 53, 1 Peter 1:20)

Though man continues to fight and kill, a Way has been made and it is up to those who know that Way to boldly and yet graciously share it with others through their words and their actions (John 13:34-35, Romans 10:9-17). Thank God, that the likes of Martin Luther, Isaac Newton, William Shakespeare, Michael Faraday, Charles Dickens, William Wilberforce, Abraham Lincoln, William and Evangeline Booth, Winston Churchill, Martin Luther King, Mother Teresa, Billy Graham, Queen Elizabeth II and countless other greats have all been positively influenced in their thoughts, words and actions by the way, the truth and the life (see: John 14:6).

> When I consider your heavens, the work of your fingers, the moon and the stars, which you have set in place, what is mankind that you are mindful of them, human beings that you care for them?

Psalm 8:3-4, see also: Psalm. 19:1-6

The Literary Master

This is the first of five historical poems recounting people and events who and which are being remembered in 2016 - their anniversary year. I utilized the celebrated words of William Shakespeare on the subjects of life and death, which can still be used as a poetic springboard over 400 years on after his passing.

I chose to write it as a pantoum (sticking to eight syllables and iambic pentameter as much as possible) as it as a form which lends itself to making the past relevant in the present. Pantoums also help the writer end the piece on an emphatic note, which resonates with many of Shakespeare's poems. I used well-known his "All the world's a stage" line, as my opening line here, but altered it for the final line so as to relay the point that if we get too tangled in the constraints of life and fail to prepare for death - life can become a 'cage', which conveniently rhymes with 'stage'.

In the Bible, St. Paul says that angels and humans watch us all the time like spectators:

> For it seems to me that God has put us apostles on display at the end of the procession, like those condemned to die in the arena. We have been made a spectacle to the whole universe, to angels as well as to human beings.

> 1 Corinthians 4:9

See 'The Bard and the Bible' near the end for more on Shakespeare and the Biblical influences on his writings.

An End to Discontent

The idea of this short piece was based around the fact that for over five centuries most historians have presented a mostly scathing version of King Richard III to which people have widely accepted. Shakespeare himself portrayed him in this way. Yet since the 2012 discovery of his body under a carpark in Leicester, the general academic and public attitude towards him has changed to a much more conciliatory one. The words of the piece might remind one of the Biblical prophecies in Psalm 22 and Isaiah 53 about the suffering, disfigurement, malignation and ridicule the coming Messiah would receive despite being completely undeserving of it.

So, I wanted to explore what Richard might think if he knew what people have been saying about him. His ears listen and his voice speaks from his unkingly and unkindly grave. The words from Henry Purcell's c. 1685 aria 'When I am laid in Earth' were chosen as the epigraph because the words are appropriate to my portrayal of Richard. He wants us to forget his so-called fate (dying as a crooked King) and instead remember the true Richard. I listened to the piece (which is used for a monarch's arrival at Remembrance services) whilst creating the poem.

I used a little archaic language in the sixth stanza only, which though often frowned upon these days, is I believe justified in order to mentally anchor the reader in the era Richard lived in. Also, in the third stanza, he refers to "strange mechanical things" above his grave. These are cars in the Leicester carpark – he wouldn't know what a car was hence that description. I gave him a partial ability to see and hear what was going on around him.

I made sure there was a simple four-line syllable grab at the end of each stanza pointedly summing up his discontent. The last lien of the final stanza has five syllables which relate to Dido's Lament. They also serve as a literary device to portray the newfound content he had sought for five hundred years. It is as though he can now rest in peace for eternity knowing his true nature has been revealed and following his more appropriate burial.

The choice of using a near-consistent number of syllables on the last line of each stanza was a subtle nod to Shakespeare's 'Richard III', who of course used the same method, but in his case, used ten to eleven syllables - and on every line! The title of this piece is also in reference to the opening line of that same play - "Now is the winter of our discontent".

The Great Fire

I based much of this on the detailed account and actions of Samuel Pepys MP (1633 - 1700), including the epigraph quoting one of his diary entries chronicling the 1666 Fire of London. The fire began in a bakery on Pudding Lane, which is the nation's oldest one-way street, having been completed in 1617 - 400 years ago (The Spectator, 2017). In keeping with the era, I included a little archaic phrasing to hopefully draw the reader back 350 years. In the sixth and seventh stanzas, I treated the word 'Parliament' as a trisyllabic word, as it is often pronounced that way.

I chose to do a rhyming 32-line piece as I felt the rhyme would give it a sense of urgency befitting the subject matter. There was also more I wanted to say than could be fitted into a simpler 16-line pantoum. Also, pantoums do not have to have a specified length. I chose to stay close to the strict tradition of having eight syllables per line.

I first attempted to write the piece as a villanelle, but found that it worked against me, so opted for a pantoum, which released the writing. I liked the repetition of whole lines, which in this case reiterate the stark elements of the disaster. I added details of my own to create more colour to the event. I appreciate how pantoums ideally attempt to close with a direct link back to the beginning. Again, this seemed appropriate for this piece as I believe it aids the reader in imagining the very real threat of that contagious fire which devoured everything in its path and destroyed such a large portion of the capital city. The fear of a raging, insuppressible fire is one of the strongest, as it is directly linked to the fear of loss (caused by unfeeling destruction); the fear of death and also the fear of receiving a hellish, tortuous death (see: Hebrews 2:14-15).

The use of 'Before them - the fire devours, behind them - a timber wood waste' was inspired by the words of the Prophet Joel, where he describes a coming war, using a (short, abrupt, broken) staccato style of poetry:

> Before them fire devours,
> behind them a flame blazes.
> Before them the land is like the garden of Eden,
> behind them, a desert waste,
> nothing escapes them.

Joel 2:3

In the same chapter, Joel describes the coming Holy Spirit, who would one day come down and empower all believers who received Him - regardless of age, race, status or gender. This was fulfilled hundreds of years after Joel's words, on Pentecost Sunday c. AD30. The Holy Spirit was poured out on the first Christians and appeared as tongues of fire. The leader of the early Christians - Peter preaches with a new fiery zeal and quotes part of Joel 2, explaining to the growing crowds that the prophecy has been fulfilled (see: Acts 2).

So, there is a fearful fire that can kill when it becomes out of control and the flames of Hell, but there is also a greater,

Godly, spiritual, refining fire of His Holy Spirit who can reside in each person's heart, helping the believer to overcome fear (see: Luke 3:16, Heb. 12). J.R.R. Tolkien called it 'the secret fire', which in his Middle Earth stories represented the Holy Spirit. It enabled Gandalf to fight the devilish fires of the underworld (Hell) (Tolkien, 1954 (2001)).

St. Paul said:

> I remind you to fan into flame the gift of God, which is in you through the laying on of my hands. For the Spirit God gave us does not make us timid, but gives us power, love and self-discipline.
>
> 2 Timothy 1:6-7

A Great Silence

We move on to an event which occurred just over 100 years ago - the 1916 Battle of the Somme. I wanted to write about how death has no favourites - the bloodiest battle in history claimed the lives of men of all classes and backgrounds. This class-wide grouping together helped to blur the social lines well established at this point.

This poem paraphrased some of the words found in the account of World War I reporter Philip Gibbs who witnessed some horrific scenes from that battle (McNab, 2014, pp.28-29). However, I portrayed the person recounting the battle as an affected soldier who struggles with seeing his friends dying around him. The soldier is now looking down and looking back from Heaven (if that were possible).

A villanelle remained the chosen form due to its strict, repetitive nature - bringing to mind the demanding rigours of being a soldier. Many soldiers gave their life for the sake of us in this war and in many others. They paid the ultimate cost, for as Jesus said, "Greater love has no one than this: to lay down one's life for one's friends." (John 15:13). He Himself willingly died out of His great love for us all (John 3:16-19, 1 Peter 3:18).

The Servant Queen

This is a sonnet-like piece of 16 lines, with rhyming couplets throughout. It isn't in iambic pentameter for much of it and so is a rather experimental poem. I believe it works well in its own right.

It is about how even the person at the pinnacle of British society, who celebrated being the longest reigning monarch in 2015, her 90th birthday in 2016, her Sapphire Jubilee in 2017 and is the most recognised woman in the world will one day die like everyone else. Though it may seem morbid to speak of her death especially in light of the celebrations in her honour, we nevertheless have to face a nation without her. The way she has lived her life (as with anyone) is what counts, and this becomes more prevalent when one is viewed for nine decades and from several critical eyes watching you from around the globe. Her death will no doubt be a very profound and emotionally difficult time for the nation and for much of the world. I hope it doesn't happen for many years to come. Long may she reign over us!

The word 'Servant' in the title is meant to contrast with the word 'Master' in the title of the Shakespeare poem. All masters and servants die as do all who are known for their mastery of a skill or servant-like nature. Her Majesty the Queen has for me displayed a very servant-like nature throughout her exceptionally long reign. She has shared her Christian faith with increasing boldness and has shared on many occasions how Christ has aided her during her long life. Indeed, Christ -

through a King Himself, said that He "did not come to be served, but to serve, and to give [my] life as a ransom for many." (Mark 10:45).

See: 'The Queen and the King' near the end for more on the Queen and her Christian faith.

A Mighty Equalling

Continuing the theme of death having no favourites, I wanted to produce a picture of life-cycles using references to the weather and the sky. I also made references to people one would associate with the distant past, such as 'ploughboys' and 'courtly Kings', in order to emphasise that despite the greater social disparity between rich and poor then, they all lived and died under the same sky. The sun shines on all and the rain falls on all (Matthew 5:45). It is appointed for all people to die and be brought equally before Christ as judge (see: Hebrews 9:27-28).

I remember looking up at the sky one day in 2016 and seeing how blank and void it looked. That somehow captured my imagination, and reminded me of how we are here one day and then gone the next - into nothingness (at least from the perspective of others). I do not believe death is the end. The 'ground' refers to being buried. The message in this piece might remind one of *Death the Leveller* by James Shirley (1596-1666), who died just over 350 years ago. His death was apparently due to fear and exposure to the Great Fire of London. Also, St. Paul's words in 1 Timothy 6:7 inspired me with this piece: "For we brought nothing into the world, and we can take nothing out of it."

I felt a villanelle would be the most suitable form as it requires regular repetition of certain lines, which can reinforce the key message as is needed here to continue the set of poems.

I altered line 18 in order to fit in the previous lines' message which overran, therefore creating more enjambment.

The Mercantile Locomotive

I was once traveling towards Lichfield by train and as always, I enjoyed the lovely fields either side. I had the carriage to myself and the chuntering sounds of the train and the surrounding landscape began to inspire me. It was a frosty, wintry morning and somehow, I started to think of the coldness outside being comparable to the coldness within people's hearts. There are those who are just on their journey comfortably making themselves richer and richer and ignoring the plight of the poor left outside working away in the harsh reality of life.

Yet, the rich and the poor still face mortality together, even if their life here is vastly different.

In this poem, they both have a voice, but there is a third voice too:

- The oppressive and never-satisfied business people of the world who chunter on with their lives and trample over the so-called 'lower' people

- The oppressed poor who suffer and are not allowed to enjoy the benefits that the world's wealthy do, yet they do they most work

- The one good businessman - only he has a free, contented individual voice.

The rich and the poor sound similar at points here because they are mutually cold and aggressive in their tone towards one another. The one good man is gentle, peaceful and clear in his speech. The train itself could be said to have its own voice, as seen in the opening stanzas which feature rhyme, alliteration, and train-like 'ch ch' sounds. I listened to train sounds before creating this piece to help me verbalise the various sounds. Rhyme mostly disappears when describing the poor, as they are not part of the rhythm of the train. However, alliteration remains, but instead is used to emphasise the repetitive, hard labour of the oppressed.

The old adage in the eighth stanza came from a made-up saying from a friend, who himself got it from his grandfather. There is a danger of allowing coldness and bitterness to linger in one's heart, which is like snow that won't thaw. It will only harden and wait for more to add to it. What is needed is someone to break the ice. The growing snow to me also represents the growing economic debt which ballooned to bursting point in the global financial crash of 2008.

The slowing of the train which begins in the twelfth stanza represents the world's economic downturns caused by the downfalls of snow. This disrupts the rhyming pattern that was established at the outset. The reference to "squelching the smoke" is about the big city's fiscal power being weakened. 'The Big Smoke' often referred to many smog-filled cities in the industrial age. The poem is reminiscent of *The Night Mail* by W.H. Auden, which features the lines:

> *This is the night mail crossing the border,*
> *bringing the cheque and the postal order,*
> *Letters for the rich, letters for the poor...*

The link did not occur to me until the latter stages of the poem's creation. Auden was a (re)convert to Christianity after abandoning it aged 13 and turning to a morally relative view of the world. It was the faith of anti-Nazi dissident Dietrich Bonhoeffer and also the horrors Auden heard of in Nazi Germany that caused him to accept that is true evil in the world. This led him to realise there must also be true goodness and an origin for both good and evil (Kirsch, 2005). Some elements of J.R.R Tolkien's *The Lord of the Rings* was a more definite an influence as he refers to the steam-rolling effect of industry destroying (the love of) the natural world.

I struggled to avoid an anti-rich / anti-business / overly political tone. I wanted to tell about the world's injustice which many would say is caused by too much concentration of money and power in certain parts of the world. Many economic drivers are good and indeed, the saviour in the story comes from the world of business himself.

He is clearly a Christ-like figure and although Christ Himself was born into humble beginnings and lived as a poor man, He was a King and "though he was rich, yet for your sake he became poor, so that you through his poverty might become rich." and indeed through Christ we become rich in faith (2 Corinthians 8:9).

He reached out to the poor and to the rich (Luke 14:13; 18:18-30, John 12:32; see also: Proverbs 22:2). He clears the snow with a sword, because He came to bring the Word of God which divides truth from deception and justice from injustice. It draws a line in the sand (or in this case - the snow) - see: Matthew 10:32-42, Ephesians 6:17 and Hebrews 4:12.

A Letter to Death

This is an attempt at imagining what a hurt, grieving person might say if they could actually write to 'Death'. This means 'Death' must be personified, hence why I referred to its look, touch and finger. In the Bible, St. Paul refers to death's 'sting' (see: 1 Corinthians 15:55-57).

John Milton's (1608-1674) allegorical *Paradise Lost* poem about the fall of man includes Death as an actual character. I stuck to roughly 10 syllables per line and as much as possible to iambic pentameter and cross rhyme apart from the rhyming couplet at the end. Although unlike many sonnets, this is not sweet and kindly, but rather an emotional expression of hurt and perhaps bitterness too. It throws a reverser on sonnets.

The Response from Death

This is what I imagined Death might say if it could communicate and reply back. I believe Death would have a tone of finality in its voice. To this end, the second line of each stanza of this piece began to become statement-like whilst I was writing it. I also tried to write it as though you cannot quite trust Death - perhaps it would be a bit conniving?

In this case, it was so Death could share *its* fear just as the aggrieved person in the previous poem shared theirs. This to me personifies it beyond the previous poem, as it can speak from its own perspective. Death has the last word in the sequence of poems, just as all people will succumb to death (Hebrews 9:27).

With Him Face to Face

In my mind's eye I could picture an aerial view of a youngish woman sleeping in a disturbed state and perhaps muttering words of regret over something, but her semi-unconscious state was making her unaware of the pain until it wakes her up and she's fully conscious of it again.

I tried to liken the waves of guilt and hurt people often experience to the merciless cold winds of winter bringing in rains which soak you to the bones. I tried to imagine the rain which you see coming down over fields in misty layers or waves to help me. I listened to Antonio Vivaldi's (1678-1741) *Winter* from *The Four Seasons* which uses pizzicato plucking of notes from high strings to evoke the icy rains of winter - like heart strings being cruelly pulled at.

The line about 'festival's fire' being over refers to the warmth of Christmas and New Year ending, and leaving you with two more months of cold, dull, depressing weather and no celebrations. You have to face the harshness of reality and the new year whether you want to or not.

As I continued to write about someone suffering in this way, I realised I still hadn't come up with a reason why she was like this - what caused it? I just allowed the reason to appear naturally, which it did - the woman's brother had been murdered and she wasn't there to help. I asked myself how I would feel and what I would do in that situation. I think I would be tempted to hide in bed and seek comfort there.

The last two stanzas in Michael Longley's (1939-) *Leaving Inishmore* referring to letting go, to hurt and to the seasons of the year inspired me greatly (Anderson, 2006). When the woman in the poem finally stops hiding from the image of her brother's frozen face and accepts what happened she is freed from *her* winter of discontent as it were. "I was blind, but now I see" is from John Newton's (1725-1807) infamous hymn *Amazing Grace*.

One might think of the many women who stayed with Jesus as He was dying and helped anoint his body, as was tradition. What a horrific sight to see Him that day, especially for his mother Mary, and yet, they would all see Him returned to life again (see: Luke 23:49-24:12).

Why Must We Betray?

Here is an historical overview of betrayal and revenge. I wanted to convey how this incessant need in people to fight back when harmed is destructive. I was concerned about sounding preachy, but I wanted to bring moral overtones to this piece as it is about major moral issues.

I chose to portray a new-born baby in an atypically dark light to convey what revenge can do to humanity. I provided well-known historical examples of betrayal and/or revenge to show that such inhumane actions and attitudes only lead to destruction - namely for the betrayer / avenger. Judas Iscariot, Guy Fawkes and Adolf Hitler being the three examples:

- Judas Iscariot - who betrayed Jesus for love of money (Matthew 10:1-4; 27:1-5, Mark 14:43-45, John 12:1-11).

- Guy Fawkes - who tried to take revenge on King James I (Nicholls, 2004).

- Adolf Hitler - who originally felt aggrieved by the Jews of his country and so betrayed them in their masses when he became leader (Hitler, 1944 (1969)).

I included quotes about Guy Fawkes from one of his contemporaries (Nicholls, 2004) and quotes from Hitler himself - although I had to paraphrase and translate his in order to maintain rhyme and rhythm (Hitler, 1944 (1969). I also included the famous line from the fictional creature Gollum in aforementioned *Lord of the Rings* book and film trilogy. He was obsessed by 'the ring of power' which corrupted him and anyone it ensnared (Tolkien, 1954, 55).

Man has regrettably shown time and again that he is incapable of solving the world's problems and learning from his countless sins. He needs a perfect Saviour to show the way and pay the penalty and wipe the slate clean. Jesus Christ was that Saviour, who taught us to follow the Golden Rule of treating people as we would want to be treated. That of course ties in with the righteous Golden Lime Tree, who has personally known 'the One' who taught it and so shares in *His* life for all eternity (see: Luke 6:31, John 5:24;13:34-35, Acts 17:30-31).

I believe that man's great propensity towards taking revenge is removed when he chooses to follow the teachings and example of Christ and show love (represented by the rose) and peace (the olive branch) to both friend and foe (Matt. 5:43-48; 22:36-40, Luke 23:33-35). The Apostle Paul said, "[if] it is possible, as far as it depends on you, live at peace with everyone. Do not take revenge, my dear friends, but leave room for God's wrath..." He continues by giving examples of how we can help our enemies and be the bigger person (Rom. 12: 14-21).

Indeed, love and peace are two of the fruits of the Holy Spirit (Gal. 5:22-23). The Spirit in this poem is portrayed as a dove, just as He appeared as such in scripture (Luke 3:21-22). When Jesus said to His followers "receive the Holy Spirit" He preceded it with the words, "peace be with you" and proceeded it with a call to forgive (John 20:21-23). That is how He wants all His followers to be like - to be at peace as much as possible, to receive and be led by His Spirit and to forgive people when they do wrong.

The Golden Lime Tree

Autumn is my favourite season and I remember when "I stepped out" one October onto my front drive and was immediately drawn in by the lime tree almost opposite me on the other side of the road. I had my notepad in my hand and instantly began writing how I felt, what I smelt, what I saw, what I heard and even what I tasted. There was such a gentle wind, yet it whipped up every now and then as it often does at that time of the year. You cannot see the wind, but you can feel it, smell a scent that it whips up, see its affect, hear its sound and even taste the atmosphere it creates. it can be a spiritual experience reminding one of the work of the Holy Spirit - the breath of God (Job 33:4, John 3:8; 20:22, Acts 2:1-4).

I felt very much at peace and started to dwell on how a tree's natural life cycle can represent a person's life:

- birth, childhood and teenage-hood = spring

- early adulthood = summer

- middle age to old age = autumn

- death = winter

However, I wanted to begin in autumn and focus on the end of life's cycle. I also wanted to convey a truth that I believe in - that spring and summer will return to the one who knows eternal life. Though they will die, yet shall they live (John

11:25). The Bible compares people to trees many times - "The fruit of the righteous is a tree of life, and the one who is wise saves lives." (Proverbs 11:30, see also: Psalm 1, Isaiah 61:3, Matt. 7:7, Luke 13:6-9, Revelation 22:14).

It can be daunting for people - namely elderly people who will soon step out of this world and into the next. I believe that older people are increasingly being shoved aside, when their greater experience and wisdom should be respected and listened to. Life can be difficult as they become less respected, physically weaker and they see culture changing faster than the seasons of the year.

I chose not to obey any well-established tenants of poetry in this piece, other than having a sequence of stanzas roughly the same in length. I created my piece from the free writing scribblings I made that wonderful October day when I stepped out...

Now I am Ready for Death

I wanted to write another experimental sonnet, and one about a person who has accepted their own mortality. Perhaps this is the same person who stepped out in the previous poem. Even though not apparent in the writing, I kept imagining the person to be a woman who has lived life to the full (John 10:10) and when young used to enjoy running by the ocean every morning. This image in my mind's eye helped shape the process.

Sonnets usually develop an idea and attempt to explore an answer after the volta. Here, the person answers why they do not fear death, but this naturally seemed to fall after the ninth line, rather than after the eighth, as is traditional. I kept to the typical 14-line sonnet, as the poetry best fitted that length. I chose to have a set number of syllables (twelve), in order to provide a level of steadiness. This can reflect the person's healthy outlook on life and acceptance of death. However, I also made it a non-rhyming piece, so there was a fluidic element - to reflect the person's joyful personality. I count the word 'companion' as having four syllables to make the line it is on twelve syllables in total. I purposefully made sure the final word of the final line was 'life' as opposed to 'death'.

Jesus died our death to save us from our sins. He said: "I am the light of the world…the resurrection…the way and the truth and the life". (John 8:12; 11:25; 14:6). If you know all that in your heart and confess Him as Lord and Saviour you will experience that light, resurrection, direction, truth and life eternal (see: Romans 10:9-15).

You will find that death is no longer your master, but your servant - for it ushers you into the presence of Christ.

When the perishable has been clothed with the imperishable, and the mortal with immortality, then the saying that is written will come true:

**'Death has been
swallowed up in victory.'
Where, O death, is your victory?
Where, O death, is your sting?"**

The sting of death is sin, and the power of sin is the law. But thanks be to God! He gives us the victory through our Lord Jesus Christ.

1 Corinthians 15:54-56
(see also: Isaiah 25:8 and Hosea 13:14)

Amen.

APPENDIX 1
The Bard and the Bible

William Shakespeare (1564 - 1616) is universally regarded as the world's greatest ever writer. He was a Midlands boy - from Stratford Upon Avon, and 2016 marked 400 years since his death. On television, at theatres, in libraries, universities and schools throughout the nation, there were several celebrations and tributes to him. He wrote 38 plays and 154 sonnets - which cover tragedy, comedy and history and describe the human condition in such profound and eloquent ways that few other writers have.

Despite the common belief that Shakespeare's writings are generally humanistic in tone, Shakespeare actually relied heavily on the stories, poetry and moral values of the Bible. He quoted and alluded to it more than any other writer of his time. He makes over 1,200 references and allusions to 36 books of the Bible - 18 from each Testament. He particularly draws on Genesis, Job, the Psalms and Matthew. In regards to Matthew - his character Hamlet says "There is a special providence in the fall of a sparrow", which draws on Jesus' words in Matthew 10:29 about how much God cares for us. The title of the comedy 'Measure for Measure' is based on Jesus' words in the Sermon on the Mount about the measure that one uses to judge another becoming the measure God will use to judge them (see: Matthew 7:2).

In addition to this, several Bible characters are directly referred to in his works: Goliath is mentioned three times; Peter and Lazarus - seven times; Samson, Solomon and the Prodigal Son - nine times; Judas - 23 times and Cain and Job - 25 times (Bragg, 2011).

Modern scholar of Renaissance writings - Peter Milward states in his book about the tragedies that many of the Bard's contemporaries often avoided making references to religious texts due to the intense political and religious impact the Reformation was having on the nation at the time. Yet according to Millward, this "did not prevent him from making full use of the Bible in dramatizing his secular sources and thus infusing into them a Biblical meaning." Shakespeare "shows the universal relevance of the Bible both to the reality of human life 'in this harsh world' and to its ideal in the heart of God."

Similarly, Steven Marx, Professor of English at Cal Poly University in California states that Shakespeare clearly had "a thorough familiarity with the Scriptures" and that the plays' references to the Bible "illuminate fresh and surprising meanings in the biblical text."

In recent years, some British university professors have lamented their students' lack of Scripture knowledge compared to students from years ago. This is because when people do not know the Bible, they struggle to grasp Shakespeare and the many other writers who drew on Scripture, such as Dickens, Milton, Keats, Defoe and the Bronte sisters (Watchlin, 2014).

It is clear that not only can the Word of God help us understand and appreciate the works of Shakespeare better, but more importantly, Shakespeare - despite been gone for 400 years, can still help us to appreciate the Word of God more in new and unexpected ways. When there are big national events such as the celebration of Shakespeare's life and influence, we can utilize that as a great starting point for sharing the Gospel. We can enlighten people on how God's Word enriched the greatest writer's works and show how relevant the Bible was and still is in our lives!

> "So shall my word be, that goeth out of my mouth: it shall not return unto me void, but it shall accomplish that which I will, and it shall prosper in the thing whereto I sent it."
>
> (Isaiah 55:11, from the Geneva Bible - the translation Shakespeare used.)

RELATED REFERENCES:

Bragg, Melvyn. (2011) *The Book of Books: The Radical Impact of the King James Bible 1611-2011*. Hodder & Stoughton.

Marx, Steven. (2000) *Shakespeare and the Bible*, Oxford University Press, p. 13

Milward, Peter. (1987) Biblical Influences in Shakespeare's Great Tragedies. Bloomington: Indiana University Press. p. 207.

Watchlin, Marie Goughnour (2014) What professors say students need to know about the Bible. Available at: https://www.washingtontimes.com/news/2014/dec/11/the-bibles-influence-what-professors-say-students-/ (Accessed: 09 November 2017)

See also:
bbc.co.uk/news/magazine-12205084 (Accessed: 24 April 2016)
biblegateway.com/blog/2013/04/shakespeare-and-the-word/ (Accessed: 24 April 2016)

Due to the high number of quotations and allusions to his works, particularly in 'The Literary Master', I have them all been grouped here:

1st and 8th Stanza - *As You Like It* [2.7.1037-40]
2nd Stanza - As You Like It [2.7.1037-40], *Hamlet* [4.5.2905]
3rd Stanza - *Hamlet* [4.5.2905], *Macbeth* [5.5.2381-82]
4th and 5th Stanzas - *Macbeth* [5.5.2381-82]
6th and 7th Stanzas - *Richard III* [3.2.63-64]

In the title of 'An End to Discontent' and in the 5th stanza of 'The Mercantile Locomotive' I refer to the opening line of Richard III [1.1.1] - "Now in the winter of our discontent".

APPENDIX 2
The Queen and the King

On 9th September 2015, her Majesty the Queen became the longest reigning monarch of the United Kingdom, having reigned for more than 63 years and seven months, which is over 23,000 days! This is even more amazing when we consider that we have had a monarchy reigning over some or all of the UK for over a thousand years.

The Queen ascended to the throne in 1952, and was crowned a year later in 1953. My line "as a symbol of her royal majesty" is a paraphrase of a line from the British coronation ceremony. As the Archbishop of Canterbury is about to place the crown on the monarch's head, he refers to it as "a sign of royal majesty". The ceremony is filled with so much Biblical symbolism. Handel's 1727 Coronation Anthem used in every ceremony since King George II contains the words:

> *Zadok the Priest, And Nathan the Prophet*
> *Anointed Solomon - King.*
> *And all the people rejoiced, and said:*
> *God save the King! Long live the King!*
> *May the King live for ever!*

That is taken directly from 1 Kings 1:38-40, where as you can see, we get the phrase 'God save the King' (or 'Queen' in Elizabeth's case) - the title of the national anthem.

During the coronation ceremony, the Archbishop tells the incoming monarch: "Receive this orb set under the Cross, and remember that the whole world is subject to the Power of…Christ, our Redeemer…" Later, the archbishop hands a Bible to the Queen saying: "Our gracious Queen, to keep your majesty ever mindful of the Law and the Gospel of God as the Rule for the whole life and Government of Christian Princes, we present you with this book, the most valuable thing that this world affords. Here is Wisdom; this is the Royal Law; these are the Lively Oracles of God" (Ratcliff, 1953).

On 21st April 2016, the Queen celebrated her 90th birthday and as of 6th February 2017 she has reigned for 65 years. Both are major milestones, as no other British monarch has ever reached that age nor reigned for so long. As you probably know, the Queen is a professing Christian and in honour of her faith and her birthday the Bible Society produced a lovely book entitled 'The Servant Queen and the King She Serves'. It inspired me to call my poem on the Queen 'The Servant Queen'.

The Bible Society's book was mentioned by a BBC commentator during the Queen's 21st April 90th Birthday walkabout. The CEO of the Bible Society, Paul Woolley, said: "This book bears witness to the Queen's faith and the centrality of her Christian faith on her life and her reign…" and his hope is that the book would become "a talking point in your neighbourhood [and] in your office" as a way to share the Christian faith with family, friends and work colleagues. (Wooley, 2015).

The Queen is in fact the patron of the Bible Society and actually wrote the forward to the book. In it she says "I have been – and remain – very grateful to you for your prayers and to God for his steadfast love. I have indeed seen his faithfulness." She continues to quote hers and her father George VI's favourite poem by Minnie Louise Haskins (1875 - 1957) about the man who stands at 'The Gate of the Year', aka 'God Knows' (1908 (1912)). Part of this was read by David Attenborough at the Thanksgiving Service in St. Paul's Cathedral for the Queen's Official 90th birthday weekend (20th - 22nd June):

> And I said to the man who stood at the gate of the year: "Give me a light that I may tread safely into the unknown."
>
> And he replied: "Go out into the darkness and put your hand into the Hand of God.
>
> That shall be to you better than light and safer than a known way."

The Queen's faith appears to have grown as a result of the struggles she and the Royal Family went through in the 1990's. Since then she has become more expressive of her faith, and most notably so during her Christmas messages:

In 1993, she said: "I am always moved by those words in St. John's Gospel… "He was in the world, and the world was made by him, and the world knew him not". We have only to listen to the news to know the truth of that. But the Gospel goes on - "But as many as received him, to them he gave the power to become the sons of God". For all the inhumanity around us, let us be grateful for those who have received him and who go about quietly doing their work and His will without thought of reward or recognition. They know that there is an eternal truth of much greater significance than our own triumphs and tragedies, and it is embodied by the Child in the Manger. That is their message of hope. We can all try to reflect that message of hope in our own lives, in our actions and in our prayers."

In 2000, she said: "To many of us our beliefs are of fundamental importance. For me the teachings of Christ and my own personal accountability before God provide a framework in which I try to lead my life. I, like so many of you, have drawn great comfort in difficult times from Christ's words and example."

In 2012, she said: "This is the time of year when we remember that God sent his only son 'to serve, not to be served'. He restored love and service to the centre of our lives in the person of Jesus Christ...The carol, 'In the Bleak Midwinter', ends by asking a question of all of us who know the Christmas story, of how God gave himself to us in humble service: 'What can I give him, poor as I am? If I were a shepherd, I would bring a lamb; if I were a wise man, I would do my part'. The carol gives the answer, 'Yet what I can I give him – give my heart'."

I am so grateful to the Queen for maintaining and displaying a solid faith in Jesus Christ for so long. I pray she will continue to grow in Him and inspire her heirs and her entire family to commit to Him daily.

In the Bible, St. Paul calls us to pray for "kings and those in authority" so that peace and godliness may prevail in the land and because it pleases our Saviour God "who wants all people to be saved and to come to a knowledge of the truth. For there is one God and one mediator between God and men, the man Christ Jesus, who gave Himself as a ransom for all..." (see: 1 Timothy 2:1-6). Jesus Christ is "the King of Kings", "the Lord of Lords", "the Prince of Peace"! (see: Isaiah 9:6; 1 Timothy 6:15-16; Revelation 19:16).

> Since [we] have flesh and blood, he too shared in [our] humanity so that by his death he might break the power of him who holds the power of death - that is, the devil - and free those who all their lives were held in slavery by their fear of death.
>
> (Hebrews 2:14-15)

AMEN!

RELATED REFERENCES:

Butcher, Catherine; Greene, Mark (2016). *The Servant Queen and the King She Serves,* produced by CPO.

Handel, George Frederick. (1727) *Zadok the Priest (as part of the Coronation Anthems)* [online] Available at: https://en.wikipedia.org/wiki/Zadok_the_Priest#Full_text (Accessed: 22 August 2016)

Haskins, Minnie Louse (1908 (1912)). *The Gate of the Year.* [online] Available at: http://www.telegraph.co.uk/comment/columnists/christopherhowse/3561497/At-the-Gate-of-the-Year.html (Accessed: 22 August 2016).

Ratcliff, Edward. C (1953). *The Coronation Service of Her Majesty Queen Elizabeth II* Cambridge University Press. [online] Available at: https://books.google.co.uk/books?id=eKY4AAAAIAAJ&pg=PA14&redir_esc=y#v=onepage&q&f=false (Accessed: 22 August 2016).

The Queen's 1993 Christmas Speech, [online] available at: https://www.youtube.com/watch?v=T9WG2WyfdVM (Accessed: 20 August 2016).

The Queen's 2000 Christmas Speech, [online] available at: https://www.youtube.com/watch?v=Ih8mpDdj94o (Accessed: 20 August 2016).

The Queen's 2012 Christmas Speech, [online] available at: https://www.youtube.com/watch?v=GJNwVKCdWR8 (Accessed: 20 August 2016).

Windsor, Elizabeth R (Queen Elizabeth II). (1947) *21st Birthday speech* (online) Available at: https://www.royal.uk/21st-birthday-speech-21-april-1947 (Accessed: 18 August 2016).

Wooley, Paul. (2015) *Queen Elizabeth reflects on God's faithfulness as the King she serves.* Available at: http://www.biblesociety.org.au/news/queen-elizabeth-reflects-on-gods-faithfulness-as-the-king-she-serves (Accessed: 22 August 2016).

Main References

Anderson, L. (2006) (ed) *Creative Writing: a workbook with readings*, page 228, Abingdon, Routledge / Milton Keynes, The Open University.

Auden, W.H. (1936) *The Night Train,* Silver Birch Press [online]. Available at: https://silverbirchpress.wordpress.com/2013/07/16/the-night-mail-poem-by-w-h-auden/ (Accessed: 17 August 2016).

Best-selling book (2020), *Guinness World Records* https://www.guinnessworldrecords.com/world-records/best-selling-book-of-non-fiction (Accessed: 28 April 2020)

Burton, Neil. (2011). *The genius of WH Auden* [online]. Available at: https://outre-monde.com/2011/01/22/the-genius-of-wh-auden/ (Accessed: 22 August 2016).

Hitler, Adolf. (1944 (1969)) *Mein Kampf*, Jaico Publishing House; 37th Jaico Impression 2007 edition.

Kirsch, Arthur (2005) Auden and Christianity. New Haven: Yale University Press.

McDonald, Charlotte (2016) *Have more famous people died in 2016?*, BBC News [online]. Available at: http://www.bbc.co.uk/news/magazine-38329740 (Accessed: 12 October 2017)

McNab, Chris. (2014) *The Book of the Poppy*, pgs. 28-29, 'Frontline Voices: Battle of the Somme', Gibbs, Peter, Stroud, The History Press.

Newton, John. (1779) *Amazing Grace*, 'Dictionary of American Hymnology'. Available at: http://www.hymnary.org/text/amazing_grace_how_sweet_the_sound (Accessed on 19 August 2016).

Nicholls, Mark. (2004) "Fawkes, Guy (bap. 1570, d. 1606)", Oxford Dictionary of National Biography (online ed.), Oxford University Press, Available at: http://www.oxforddnb.com/index/9/101009230/ (Accessed: 28th May 2015).

Pepys, Samuel. (1666) *Diary of Samuel Pepys - September 5th entry* (online) Available at: http://www.pepys.info/fire.html (Accessed: 18 August 2016).

Purcell, Henry. (c. 1685) *Dido's Lament* [online]. Available to listen to at: http://www.classicfm.com/composers/purcell/music/dido-and-aeneas/#akgu1Wd4rMlOP8P3.97 (Accessed: 19 August 2016).

Sagan, Carl. (1994) *Pale Blue Dot*, The Planetary Society [online] Available at: http://www.planetary.org/explore/space-topics/earth/pale-blue-dot.html (Accessed: 28 May 2015).

Tennyson, Lord Alfred. (1849) *In Memoriam A.H.H.* The Literature Network [online] Available at: http://www.online-literature.com/tennyson/718/ (Accessed: 18 August 2016).

The Spectator. (2017) *2017's forgotten anniversaries* [online]. Available at: http://blogs.spectator.co.uk/2017/01/2017s-forgotten-anniversaries/ (Accessed: 14 Feb 2017)

Tolkien, J.R.R. (1954) *The Fellowship of the Ring*, pp. 433-434, HarperCollinsPublishers, Hammersmith, London, Film tie-in edition, 2001.

Here is the link to the scene where Gandalf battles the fiery, demonic Balrog who came from the underworld:
https://www.youtube.com/watch?v=Y2fweOrnHak

Tolkien, J.R.R. (1954/55) *The Lord of the Rings,* (based on the 50th Anniversary Single volume edition 2004), HarperCollins; Reprint edition (5 June 2007).

Nicholson, William. (1993) *The Shadowlands* (1993) Richard Attenborough, Sony Pictures, Paramount Pictures.

Wordsworth, William. (1804) *I Wandered Lonely as a Cloud,* [online]. Available at: https://www.poetryfoundation.org/poems-and-poets/poems/detail/45521 (Accessed: 19 August 2016).

Some of the many famous and influential people who died in 2016

There was an usually high number of deaths of the rich and the famous in 2016. So noted by many news organisations across the world, including the BBC, who reported that there were double the amount of celebrity deaths in 2016 compared to 2015 and five times more than in 2012 (McDonald, 2016).

David Bowie	Kenny Baker
Alan Rickman	Gene Wilder
Terry Wogan	Shimon Peres
Harper Lee	Jean Alexander
Nancy Reagan	Sir Jimmy Young
Frank Sinatra Jr	Robert Vaughn
Paul Daniels	Fidel Castro
Ronnie Corbett	Jimmy Perry
David Gest	John Glenn
Victoria Wood	Andrew Sachs
Prince (Rogers Nelson)	Zsa Zsa Gabor
Muhammed Ali	George Michael
Jo Cox	Richard Adams
Anton Yelchin	Carrie Fisher
Caroline Ahern	Debbie Reynolds

THE GOSPEL

There is nothing quite like the pain of losing a loved one. It can sometimes seem unjust of God to allow those whom we love and look up to, to just die ~ especially when it happens unexpectedly. It was actually never His intention for people to suffer or die. God's Word tells us from the start that God made a good world and that suffering and death entered the world due to man's rebellion of God. As a result of man's fall from grace, the consequences of suffering and death affected all generations since. Man's desire to turn away from God is called sin in the Bible, which means to miss the mark and to fall short of God's holy standard.
(Genesis 3, Romans 3:23; 5:12)

As most people accept, there should be consequences to doing wrong. Because God is sinless, pure and just He cannot allow sin to go unpunished for ever. But because people's sinful mistakes often have unfair consequences on others and because we could not save ourselves from the weight of our own sins, God in His mercy provided a way for all people to be saved from their sins. He saw that we were destroying ourselves ~ so just at the right time, He sent His one and only Son to become like one of us - to become a man and to show us the way back to Him.
(John 1:1-14; 3:16-17, Romans 5:6, Titus 1:1-2, 1 Peter 3:18)

Jesus was His name and He had the final say on sin, suffering and death. As a perfect human being ~ He was the only one in history who could take our sin away ~ the very thing that separated us from a sinless God.

Because suffering and death are the consequences of sin, Jesus humbly allowed Himself to suffer the worst possible death, by being nailed to a wooden cross. He did no wrong, yet was treated like a criminal. He took our place.
Yet on the third day He rose again from the grave, pushing back its power over Him and this meant He is able to offer anyone who believes in Him eternal life. He ascended back to God the Father and now intercedes for us on our behalf.
(Colossians 1:15-23; 2:13-15, Hebrews 7:24-25, 1 Peter 2:24)

Through our acknowledgment and confession of sin ~ the power of Jesus Christ's selfless sacrifice and resurrection becomes effective in our lives and we are freed from sin's power. We will still experience suffering and will ultimately die physically, but we shall live with Him forever. Because of our new life in Him, we can boldly approach His throne without fear of reproach or rejection.
(John 11:25, 1 John 1: 8-9; Hebrews 4:15-16)

When we choose to follow Jesus Christ He sends us His Holy Spirit to live inside of us and show us how to be more like Him. As we allow ourselves to be led by Him, He gently helps us to turn from sinfulness and gives us wisdom, counsel and comfort. One day, we will enter eternity and live with God our Father and Creator, where there will be no more sin, suffering or death. Jesus has promised to return in order to judge the world and bring peace to this ever-troubled world.
He will find us innocent, so long as we remain in Him.
(John 14-16; Revelation 21-22)

That is the Gospel according to God's Word,
I hope you read it and believe in it.

Why not turn away from your old life and believe in Jesus today…Ask Him to help you and forgive you.

I know that He will!

If you made that commitment then why not start reading God's Word - the Bible.
Look at the Gospels, which record the life, death and resurrection of Christ.

Ask God to help you find a good Bible-believing, God-fearing church and commit yourself to His service in His Kingdom.

Notes

Notes

Notes

Notes

OTHER WORKS BY THE AUTHOR

GOSPEL POETRY: Book 2 highlights the issue that affects everyone - loneliness. From the young to the old and from the rich to poor, no one is immune. And it appears to be a growing problem.

The expressive and creative nature of poetry - in all its many forms can be used to describe the human condition in ways not always possible with straight words and dialogue. Many poems throughout the millennia have vividly expressed pain, suffering and loneliness.

Screenwriter and playwright William Nicholson once said: "We read to know we are not alone" (1993). There is something about reading someone else's words which helps us know we are not the only ones grappling with difficult emotions and painful circumstances.

The writings of the Book of Psalms in the Bible cover every possible emotion and experience that a person can go through. Many have sought solace in the Psalms and have found comfort and counsel through their very honest and wise words. The reading of many other sources of poetry can also potentially help those suffering from the plight of unwanted solitude.

So, this second Gospel Poetry book tries to highlight this issue of lonesomeness and then present the solution - God's offer of perfect friendship. This solution is found in the Psalms and throughout the Bible and it is the writer's belief that it is the same solution to all of man's many problems.

OTHER WORKS BY THE AUTHOR

The Holy Spirit is the least understood person of the Trinity and yet the Bible says that He has been given to all believers to guide them throughout their Christian walk.

This book has been written as an encouragement to all followers of Christ to pray for a renewal of their expectancy for God the Holy Spirit to work in their lives, their church and throughout this nation.

It explores the Bible to see who the Holy Spirit is and to show why He is the much-needed counsellor and comforter for all people living in the 21st century.

It has been dedicated to two Spirit-led, Spirit-filled Christian men - Paul Miller (1949-2015) and Ray Granner (1929-2015), who did so much for spreading the truth of Gospel in Birmingham and beyond.

'The Holy Spirit' by Ciaran Thompson, released on the one year anniversary of Paul Miller's passing - 14th October 2016, is available in eBook and paperback form from Amazon.co.uk.

Printed in Great Britain
by Amazon